AF440138

LORENZO PECCHIONI - ENIO PECCHIONI

DANTE

AND HIS NEIGHBOURHOOD IN

FLORENCE

PRESS & ARCHEOS

FROM THE TEXT OF THE DOCUMENTARY
"FIORENDIPITÀ"
(*FLORENDIPITY*)
UPDATED ACCORDING TO NEW RESEARCH
FLORENCE 2019

Edizioni Press & Archeos
via Cittadella, 9 50144 Florence Italy
http://www.pressandarcheos.com
info@pressandarcheos.com

*Ma quello ingrato popolo maligno
Che discese di Fiesole ab antico,
E tiene ancor del monte e del macigno,*

*Ti si farà, per tuo ben far, nimico:
Ed è ragion; che tra li lazzi sorbi
Si disconvien fruttare al dolce fico.*

(…) But that
ungrateful, wicked people, which of old
came down from Fièsole, and which e'en now
smacks of the mountain and of hard grey stone,

for thy well-doing shall become thy foe;
and rightly, for among the acid sorbs
it is not fitting that sweet figs bear fruit.

INFERNO XV, 61-66

FIRENZE - Casa ove nacque il Divino Poeta Dante Alighieri.

Introduction

Every city has a historic centre, and every historic centre has a place or monument that can be considered its "heart". The "heart of the city" speaks to visitors about a decisive or essential historical event and is often associated with an important citizen, sometimes a religious, or a legendary figure. Citizens can ideally go to the "heart" of the historic centre to reflect and contemplate, to rediscover a connection with themselves and the roots of their identity, to draw energy from the past.

If we take the case of Florence, we can see that there are a multitude of equally important places and characters. However, Florentines who want to see themselves reflected in a historical figure or monument will be spoilt for choice. Here we have such emblematic figures as Lorenzo, Leonardo, Cosimo, Michelangelo, Arnolfo, Filippo Brunelleschi and many others.

But if it is true that the greatest Italian scholar of all times is Dante Alighieri, and if it is true that his Commedia has even been elevated to a sacred level, then the "heart" of the city could well be "his home": what we know as Piazza Dante, with the Museum, the nearby church, the tower-houses, the charming alleys, the Badia and the houses surrounding it.

However, the readers, perhaps Florentine themselves, will notice that they do not know many citizens capable of having a "heartfelt" relationship with Dante's Quarter. On the contrary, the originality of some of the architectural reconstructions is often criticised. Be that as it may, the area does not seem to be one of the most representative of the city.

Why has the ideality of the "Quartiere Dantesco" not been imposed on the Florentines, as it has been in similar cases in other great cities? Is it really possible that the issue of the exile of the Poet, rejected by the city in 1302/1304, still weighs? But those streets, those monuments, those figures, those "lazzi sorbi"[1] were in any case sung by Dante (who lived there from 1265 until his exile), transcending them into a dimension as restless as it was sublime. The soul of the Poet was and is here above all else!

Perhaps a century ago the relationship between Dante and the Florentines was different, more intense and more pronounced. And perhaps, in our time, certain ideal relationships have lost a little of their lustre everywhere, so much so that we do not necessarily have to speak of a specifically Florentine case. But even from these initial considerations it is clear how the in-depth study of Dante and his original Rione raises some questions about the soul of the Florentines and their relationship with their history; about the oversimplification of tourist sites that deserve sophisticated attention.

So if we visit the Rione today with the intention of keeping a lively and open eye on the symbolic meaning of the events that have taken place here, we may find that we do not know enough: that we have taken much for granted. And we may feel the need to learn more about places and events that have contributed so much to the

---

[1] INFERNO, XV, 65.

construction of our imagination, even if they remain largely "literary" today.

It may seem necessary, in short, to feel like starting from scratch, overcoming prejudices, in search of new barycentres.

The research contained in this book corresponds precisely - and simply - to such a restart and retracing. It was born on the inevitably synthetic and illustrative track of the text of a video documentary published years ago, with many necessary insights.

Like any research, it was born of the need to dig into oneself, to shed light on a shadowy area, to refine details that had only been sketched; to release, step by step, a written synthesis that is the solution and the saturated imprint of a journey.

Entrance to the Quartiere Dantesco from Via del Corso

Dante's Neighbourhood

When we speak of the "Rione di Dante" or the "Quartiere Dantesco", we are referring to a maze of narrow streets with more or less precise boundaries, a few blocks in the medieval heart of the city of Florence. It is here that you will find the greatest concentration of plaques commemorating Alighieri and his poetry. The streets link a few places or monuments that can be traced back to the Poet, his family or the characters that appear in his literary works.

In fact, the toponym (if one can speak in such terms) is of recent origin: the "Dante's Neighbourhood" or "Dante's District" certainly did not belong to Dante or the Alighieri family, although, as we shall see, their houses were located in several places.

The entrance to the Rione

Traditionally, the entrance to Dante's Rione is through an arch that opens onto Via del Corso. On either side of the entrance to the vault are two large shelves with pontaie holes: the building is nothing more than the base of one of the Cerchi towers, transformed into a passageway gallery.

If you are one of those who need silence and solitude to get in touch with the "soul of a place", we suggest you go to Dante's neighbourhood very early in the morning, when the shops are still closed and most of the tourists are still in their hotels. In the hours that follow, these alleys will be full of people and noise, while the open shop shutters may reveal activities that are not always in keeping with the historical imagination.

Be that as it may, walking through the alleys, still deserted or crowded with busy Florentines and fascinated tourists, it is normal to be overcome by a feeling of deep respect for the supreme Poet and all that he represents. Our schooling, our fathers and grandfathers, but also the cinema and the books, have instilled in us a sense of reverence, almost awe, for Dante and for the places of his real and literary events.

These feelings were still very much alive in the middle of the 19th century, when the project to identify and highlight a "Dante House" was born, and the history of the Dante's Neighborhood as it is today began.

Fresco of the Annunciation inside the vault
known as "of St. Margaret's or "of the Giuochi"

Archaeology of the Dante's District

This part of Florence has very ancient origins and some archaeological stratification. The Corso corresponds to the ancient Decumanus Maximus, one of the two main routes of the Roman road chessboard. A few meters to the east, on Via del Proconsolo, were the city walls, a section of which can be seen inside the Palazzo delle Mura Romane.

The medieval buildings rested on very ancient structures, perhaps corresponding in part to the Roman domus, which were distributed along the city's road system, in residential insulae bounded by the minor cardi and decumani. It can be said that the Dantesque district, rather than being a district or a single square, corresponds to some of these insulae, in which the buildings took forms and arrangements related to the natural human needs, daily life and traditions of the people.

No archaeological excavations have ever been carried out in relation to Dante Alighieri, as was the case, for example, with Lisa Gherardini or some of the Medici. Documentary research has been preferred in order to clarify the situation of this insula in the 14th century.

The Ancient Circle

In Dante's Insula we fare in the heart of what Dante called the Cerchia antica, which corresponds to the city walls built in the 12th century, when the city was at the beginning of its economic boom.[2] In the first half of the 14th century, the "circle" was further widened.

In the central canto of Paradiso, Dante tells us about his Florence. It is generally believed that this Florence is the product of Dante's poetry, but it is significant that Alighieri wants to evoke an idea of an ancient city. And this idea is projected into the future, referring to the city to which the Poet would like to return.[3] As if to say that it is impossible to imagine a future without rediscovering the past.

The ancient city, with its housing units, districts or insulae, but also with its human values, is thus both a physical place and a place of the soul, where reality and utopia can caress each other. It is from this feeling that the essence of a programme for the Future is drawn.

In this sense, the reconstructions of the capital, Florence, although probably necessary for urbanistic and purely hygienic reasons, have undoubtedly demolished, in addition to houses, a multitude of specificities, peculiar forms of subsistence, social and cultural realities, whose heritage is now irretrievably lost.

The insula or "rione" is the smallest unit of an urban reality that still has defensive walls, that is to say an identifiable and guarded city, with a psychology that is quite different from that perceived by today's citizens. It is not easy to imagine it today the reality of the ancient quarter.

---

[2] Paradiso, XV, 97-129.

[3] Based on the observations of L. Conti Lapi, interviewed in the documentary *Fiorendipità, history and soul of the Rione di Dante*, Mediaframe, Florence 2013.

A glimpse of Via Dante Alighieri

In the second half of the nineteenth century, the Florentine historian Guido Carocci tells us about the first attempt to identify Dante's house and to create a collection of Dante's relics.[4] The proponent was Lord George John Warren Vernon, who in 1841 obtained a concession from the City Council to put up a plaque identifying the building at 2 Via Dante Alighieri (formerly Via San Martino) as the Alighieri house where "the divine Poet was born". But the house, with its modest features, did not live up to patriotic expectations, and already Carocci argued that it was time to «dispel (...) that belief which is fed by a modern inscription».[5]

Inside the house, Lord Vernon, an eccentric character who is said to have dressed up as Dante himself, had collected various objects related to Dante's imagery and many valuable editions of the Comedy.

At that time, it was probably thought that the Alighieri family had more luxurious residences, and attention was focused on the buildings adjacent to the small museum, then on the site of the present house, where popular tradition and some documents from the parish of Santa Margherita pointed to a Dante tower1 [6] or other buildings belonging to the Poet's family.

It is curious that many years later, when the

---

[4] G. Carocci, *La casa di Dante*, in Arte e Storia, XX, 1891, 24, pp. 153-155.

[5] Ibid., p. 154.

[6] The information comes from G. Richa, who casts doubt on the coincidence between that tower and the house of Alighieri, in *Notizie istoriche delle chiese fiorentine*, t. II, lezione XIII.

historiographical work seems to have been completed, centuries later, attention is once again being paid to the location of the much-discussed plaque, which was visible until 1911.

The House Research Commission

In 1864, in anticipation of Dante's centenary and of becoming the capital of Italy, Florence thought of doing something very patriotic by restoring a house museum to Dante's memory. The city council decided to buy the buildings that had belonged to the Poet's family as a matter of priority,[7] with the intention of recovering the walls, restoring them and, if necessary, rebuilding them in an appropriate style. There would certainly have been no shortage of funds for a project of such symbolic importance.

It was necessary, however, to determine which of the houses mentioned by popular rumour or by some remote source could really be linked to the Alighieri and Dante. For this reason, a Commission for Research on Dante's House was set up, composed of the lawyer Emilio Frullani, Professor Gaetano Bianchi, Luigi Passerini and Mariano Falcini.

The commission took about two years to present its research in a Report that was read to the City Council on 10 March 1868. In it they attempted a reconstruction of the history of the house for which Dante's sons Jacopo and Piero came to compromise with their uncle

---

[7] General Council of the Municipality of Florence, meeting of 4 February 1865.

Francesco in 1332[8]. The Commission's research, rich in insights but, according to many, premeditated and not always impeccable, points definitively to Dante's houses on a property with a fragmented history, located in Piazza San Martino, "facing the Torre della Castagna", but also facing Via Santa Margherita.

The present Dante House

---

[8] AA. VV., *Della Casa di Dante. Relazione con documenti al consiglio generale del comune di Firenze*, Successori Le Monnier, Florence 1865. We will call it *Report* from now on. Cfr. Piranesi, *Le Case degli Alighieri*, Lumachi, Firenze 1905, pp. 20-21.

The tower house incorporated into the present Dante House

The (re)construction of the buildings

Negotiations began immediately for the purchase of the Alighieri houses, but the project was delayed by the further transfer of the capital to Rome.

It was not until 1911 that the work began, entrusted to the architect Giuseppe Castellucci, who first demolished part of the buildings, creating the small square we see today, and then rebuilt the current Casa Dante on the remains of the old houses. The new building also incorporated one of the two towers of the Giuochi family, to whom a neighbouring square is dedicated.

The house was equipped with typical fourteenth-century architectural solutions, such as projecting corbels and pontaie holes, and a choreographic well. The external masonry presents the typical "filaretto" solution of the medieval suggestion.

On the outside there is a sculptural bust of Dante by Augusto Rivalta. It seems that this is not the only representation of the Poet in the square: on a slab of the floor there is a sketch of a profile of Dante, sculpted by an unknown author.

Inside the Museum of Dante's House there are numerous medieval artefacts and educational itineraries that introduce the personal and literary history of Dante and the world of medieval Florence.

*Introduction to the research
on the houses of the Alighieri*

Locating the house in which the Poet lived or was born is a complex matter, involving the study of notarial, cadastral and biographical documents.

Approaching the details of the topic, one gets the impression that the inspiration for the research affected only a few souls (In fact, there are not that many books dedicated to it), attracted by a subject that, in a short time, seemed too materialistic compared to the existential breadth of Alighieri's legacy. What does it matter where Dante was actually born, given the literary monuments he has left us? The mere consideration of this question can be considered unproductive and, as we shall see, dangerously shrouded in particular historiographical complexity. It is also for these reasons that, with the passage of time, opinions on the reality of the house have tended to level off.

Rather than examining the archival-historiographical dimension, in this contribution we will recount the main features of the history of the aforementioned research and its protagonists, and then, why not, turn to other symbolic horizons.

At the heart of research

In order to understand the breadth and fascination of the research on Dante's real home, it is necessary to immerse oneself in it, and it is undeniable that we often glimpse certain prejudices related to the needs, affiliations and politics of individuals and organisations. This was already evident in the early days of of the investigation of the Dante's Neighborhood, when it was absolutely necessary to determine where the house should be rebuilt, but not only then.

There is undoubtedly an additional aspect to be taken into account, especially for publications from the late nineteenth and early twentieth centuries. Some research seems to want to be closely associated with a form of sacredness. At one time, this value was expressed in the importance of identifying "native walls" capable of attracting energy, if not even preserving lost secret objects or manuscripts. It is a phenomenon linked to the symbolic power of the hero. For example, as in the case of a character like Garibaldi.

The walls of Dante's house are perhaps for some a metaphor for that which is eternally elusive, linked to the mystery of the existence of great men and a destiny of redemption. They are nothing, just stone and lime, but for that very reason they invite us to reflect on the absolute merits of the best men.

Houses related to the presence of the Alighieri family
in Piazza San Martino

If Dante himself, in some passages of the Commedia, hinted at the place of his dwelling, attributing to it an ideal importance (perhaps as a "cradle" of the values of the Ancient Circle[9]) already his earliest biographers attempted a determination of the places where such "energies" could be remembered.

But even before the Poet's own existence, there are important historical references to the family of which Dante was the sublime fruit. In the first half of the twentieth century, this material was taken up, expanded and elaborated in three or four important publications, the cornerstones of which were the often ambiguous archival-catastral documents.

Thus, around Dante's house, there is a subtle but intense, reserved but surprising question, capable of reappearing periodically in current Florentine events, or at least in the souls of some Florentines. And here we are, today, still here.

What do Dante's early biographers tell us?

In order to follow the traces of the houses where the Poet was probably born and where his father and grandfather probably lived, we can refer to his early biographers.

In particular, Leonardo Bruni, chancellor of the Florentine Republic at the turn of the 14th and 15th centuries, writes in his *Life of Dante* that "...the Messer

---

[9] In the *Commedia* it is the spirit of Cacciaguida, Dante's ancestor who died in the Holy Land, who evokes an ancient Florence purer in values (PARADISO, XV, 97-129).

Cacciaguida, called Alighieri, lived on the [«in su la»] piazza behind San Martino del Vescovo, in front [«dirimpètto»] of the road that leads to the Sacchetti house…".[10]

The houses of the Sacchetti family, traditional enemies of the Alighieri family, were located at the corner of Via de' Magazzini and Garbo, now Via Condotta. In the fifteenth century Alamanno Rinuccini confirms the memory of the presence of the Alighieri, who lived «dreto a San Martino del Vescovo dirimpetto alla via che va a casa de' Sacchetti e a casa de'Rinuccini», and "on the other side stretched out near the houses of the Donati and the Giuochi families".[11]

In the text of the Report of 1865 we read that "it is a fact that the house of the Poet was in the people of SanMartino and looked over the square, as noted by every ancient document and more particularly by the authority of Leonardo Bruni himself, who led there to see the nephew of it Dante, in his passage through Florence".[12]

Others, after Bruni, will report the information,[13] and Giuseppe Richa will clearly conclude that "in this square was Dante's house, inhabited by him and by those he left

---

[10] Leonardo Bruni, *Vita di Dante*, Firenze 1436.

[11] The episode is recalled on several occasions by late nineteenth-century researchers, as in AA. VV., *The House of Dante Alighieri in Florence. Report of the Commission established by the Municipal Council of March 17, 1866 for the completion of historical research on the same*, Successori Le Monnier, Firenze 1869, p. 9.

[12] It is reiterated in the *Report*, p. 3.

[13] For a brief examination see G. Piranesi, *Le case degli Alighieri*, cit. pp. 6-8. Piranesi also recalls a document from 1550 in which a «via rincontro alla Casa di Dante» is mentioned, mistakenly identifying this street with the Piazzetta dei Giuochi, when in fact it is Via de' Magazzini. M. Barbi-R. Piattoli, *La Casa di Dante*, in *Studi Danteschi*, vol. XXII, Sansoni, Florence 1938, p. 66.

when he went into exile".[14]

Reading these memoirs, it seems that the houses of the Alighieri who were closest to Dante, and of Dante himself, were considered, already a few decades after the Poet's death, to be located roughly in correspondence with a part of the present house museum.

Technical overview of the Alighieri houses
published in the Report of 1865

---

[14] G. Richa, cit., t. 11, lez. XIII, cfr. Piranesi, *Le case degli Alighieri*, cit. p. 12.

The building corresponding to no. 2 Via Dante Alighieri

The problem of the location of Dante's house. An attempt at synthesis

The Report of 1865

We now come to the complex building situation of the houses that were recovered and undermined by the 19th century renovations to make way for today's Dante's House. According to the well-known 1869 Report, these houses, including the dilapidated tower known to the people as "Dante's Tower", together with other houses facing Via Santa Margherita, were inhabited by the Alighieri family.

The Commission's researchers focused on two dwellings. One facing the Torre della Castagna (corresponding to house no. 2 in via Dante Alighieri, at that time owned by the 'Mannelli-Galilei' family) and the other slightly to the right (owned by the Campani family)[15], both roughly coinciding with the south-western part of today's Casa di Dante.

From the historical sources, it seemed logical to identify the buildings with a property that Piero, son of Dante, ceded to Orsanmichele in 1344. It was known that this property was the result of a division made in 1332 between Dante's sons and their uncle Francesco (we will deal with this source in detail[16]).

In fact, the study of a document dated 1370, in which

---

[15] *Report*, pp. 9 e 13.

[16] Ibid., p. 43 (doc. X).

the owners of the house "on the left" regulated the distribution of light and water with one of their neighbours, a certain Niccolò di Lapo Biliotti[17], heir to the Mardoli family, led to the suspicion that these houses were part of a single original building. The Architect Falcini, under the pressure of a new warrant from the Municipality (20 March 1866), had access to the houses for a direct investigation and brought back valid elements from which to deduce the unity of the layout and communication of the buildings, bricked-up windows or doors, etc.[18]

In the meantime, the historical research into the boundaries of the properties and the names of the families involved indicated the possibility that the Biliotti property, which was already linked to other cadastral parcels affected by the current Casa Muse[19], corresponded to the 'Campani' house.

The need for the "second warrant" was obviously to reach a conclusion, and with some urgency the researchers compiled and published a final set of documents and Falcini's report.

After a series of corrections to the text of the Report, for "critical considerations that were considered inappropriate to the subject",[20] Gargano Gargani resigned from the commission in indignation. Giorgio

---

[17] Between the owner of the property and the Rector of the Chapel of Santa Margherita (who succeeded Arrighi by ecclesiastical benefice) and Niccolo Biliotti. *Report*, p. 70 (doc. n. VI).

[18] AA. VV., *La Casa di Dante Alighieri in Firenze. Relazione della Commissione istituita dalla Giunta Municipale del 17 marzo 1866 per compimento delle ricerche storiche sulla stessa*, cit., p. 8.

[19] The history of these properties has been described by M. Barbi-R. Piattoli in *La Casa di Dante*, cit., pp. 23 e seg.

[20] G. Piranesi, *Le case degli Alighieri*, cit., p. 36.

Piranesi testifies that there was no great sympathy between Gargani and the poet Emilio Frullani, the most influential member of the Commission. It was the latter who read the Report to the Commune in August 1869.[21]

Eventually, rumours began to circulate that the two scholars were not convinced by their own research, which had been carried out in such a short time.[22]

Piranesi's research: Geri's House

Many of the conclusions presented in the Report were strongly questioned by Giorgio Piranesi, who, in addition to looking at other historical sources, concentrated on the individual documents presented by the Commission, pointing out one by one the 'misstatements' and approximations. We are at the beginning of the 20th century, almost forty years after the Report was presented. Years during which a certain unease might have developed about the reality of the place where Dante lived.

A fundamental point of Piranesi's refutations concerns the dwelling of Geri di Bello Alighieri, who was mistakenly considered to be Dante's father (he was actually his father's cousin) at the time of the Commission's investigations and much later.[23]

---

[21] G. Piranesi, *Le case degli Alighieri*, cit., p. 36.

[22] Ibid., cit., p. 10.

[23] The idea that Dante was the son of Geri, also advocated by D. Bortolan in his essay dedicated to Geri (*Geri del Bello*, Ex-Cordelia, Venice 1864), was demolished by Barbi in a review (M. Barbi, *Domenico Bortolan, Geri del Bello*, in *Bullettino della Società Dantesca Italiana*, v. II, 1895, henceforth *Recensione a Bortolan*, p. 68) that would inspire further observations by Piranesi. The crux of the

According to an appraisal document of 1269, [24] included among the papers attached to the Report, Geri lived in a house "aliquantulum destructam" (undone, yes, but not destroyed[25]), bordering on the Donati family, the Mardoli family and Bellincione Alighieri (Dante's grandfather). This is still near the house museum, but now that it is clear that Dante's father was not Geri,[26] Piranesi casts serious doubt on the Poet's birth in that exact place.

Furthermore, the boundaries of the property in the document do not sufficiently correspond to those described in the aforementioned document of the purchase by Dante's sons of half of the house that also belonged to Francesco Alighieri (whose boundaries are: Donati-Ticci-Giammori, Cocchi, Mardorli). So, the researcher concludes that "either the house of 1269 is the same as the one of 1332, and then (...) Dante was not born there; or it is not the same, and we must no longer speak of it".[27]

---

matter perhaps lies in the fact that "Geri" was also Alighiero's nickname, as is unequivocally clear from a parchment of 1309 («...presentibus testibus vocatis et rogatis Francischo Allagherii dicto ser Geri», ibid., p. 67-68), already forwarded, with a simplification error, by Gargani (cfr. *Report*, p. 40). It is specified that Dante himself is called «de Allegheriis» in two sources and his half-brother «olim Alagherii». There remains some obscurity as to why Dante's father had for a nickname the same baptismal name as his quarrelsome cousin, a "schismatic" and for some a "falsifier" (ibid. p. 69), as well as a sower of discord (INFERNO, XXIX, 13-39); and whose closest relatives were perhaps already living in the "distant" via de' Cimatori.

[24] G. Piranesi, *Le Case degli Alighieri*, cit., pp. 19 e 21., cfr. *Relazione*, p. 32 (doc. n. 4).

[25] G. Piranesi, *Le Case degli Alighieri*, cit. p. 53.

[26] Ibid., p. 13.

[27] Ibid., p. 22.

Piazza San Martino in a night-time view

Piranesi went on to examine the documents submitted by the Commission, some of which were in fact unnecessary, and claimed that the Commission had carried out its research in a "wonderfully brief" manner and even in an atmosphere of internal conflict. There were rumours, for example, that Gargani was not very familiar with Latin,[28] which was certainly significant for the time and circumstances.

Piranesi also focuses on a very specific source, which tells us about a tree.

[28] G. Piranesi, *Le Case degli Alighieri*, cit., p. 10.

The Alighiero's fig tree

On the 9th of December 1189, the priest Tolomei, rector of San Martino, obtained from the sons of Cacciaguida «Preitenittus et Alighieri» an undertaking to cut down a fig tree that apparently occupied part of the land of the church and caused some nuisance.[29]

It was Giorgio Piranesi who seriously considered this source, hitherto remembered with curiosity or little more, in order to understand the location of at least part of the Poet's family property.

On the basis of this document, we must assume that the garden of the house of Alighiero I, Dante's great-grandfather, was adjacent to that of the church, which at that time, as we shall see, faced in the opposite direction to the present Oratory. Unfortunately, the source does not clarify whether the tree was on the edge of the property or whether there was a boundary wall. What is mentioned, however, is the cutting down of the plant («penitus abscident et extirpabunt») and not the cutting off of a few branches[30]; instead, in the past, there was a widespread "supposition, invention" that the problem was simply the leafy branches that blocked the air and light.[31]

According to Piranesi, it was a question of boundaries: the tree was on church property and should not be

---

[29] G. Piranesi, *Le case degli Alighieri*, p. 16, cfr. *Report,* p. 29 (doc. n. III); dall'*Archivio Diplomatico Fiorentino*, from Badia Fiorentina.

[30] Anna Franchi, *Le case degli Alighieri*, in *La Lettura*, a. XXI, n. 10, ottobre 1921, pp. 744-745.

[31] G. Piranesi, *Le case degli Alighieri*, cit., p. 16.

there.[32] This is confirmed by another source, dated 13 November 1189, in which the parish priest lodged a complaint against two men, Folle and Bencivenni, who "unjustly kept a fig tree on the land of the aforementioned church".[33] Were there more figs? The point is that in this second case, a trespassing problem is clearly evident.

In short, according to Piranesi, it is probable that Alighiero and Preitenitto had a property on the other side of the apse of the church of San Martino and that they 'trespassed' from there; that their original residence was therefore not on the northern side of via di San Martino, where the homes of Dante's closest relatives were located, and where the Casa Museo stands. In fact, these are and were divided by a road[34] and it is therefore difficult to imagine that boundary problems such as those described above could arise.

The ancient Via de' Cimatori and the house of Cione di Bello

Piranesi therefore focused his attention on the area to the left of the façade of the current church, far beyond Via di San Martino (now Via Dante Alighieri, as mentioned above), concentrating on other Alighieri whose writings had appeared in those years.[35]

---

[32] G. Piranesi, *Le case degli Alighieri*, cit., p. 16.

[33] Ibid., p. 16-17, cfr. *Report*, p. 30-31 for the full text.

[34] This is confirmed by a source from September 1277 that speaks of a «viam pubblicam lastricatam» on that side of the church. G. Piranesi, *Le case degli Alighieri*, cit., p. 17.

[35] See M. Barbi, *Recensione a Bortolan*, pp. 65 e seg.

In 1295, according to a notarial deed preserved in the Florence State Archives, Cione di Bello, a cousin of Dante's father, redeemed the property confiscated from his son Lapo for his participation in the attack and sacking of the Palazzo del Comune. This property consisted of the sixteenth part of two buildings bordering the Cerchi property and the Badia Fiorentina property. We are therefore in the area of today's Via de' Magazzini.[36]

A little later, on 7 January 1297, a petition was sent to the "Ufficiali Preposti alle Strade". The document requested the opening of a new road from the so-called "platea Orti Sancti Michelis" to the "Palatium Comunis et Populi Florentini"[37]. The Palazzo del Comune was then what was to become the Bargello. The road was to start from the houses in front of Orsanmichele, cross the loggia and Piazza dei Cerchi, and reach what is now Via del Proconsolo. It was to go, we read, "as far as the street that stands in front of the house of the Cerchi and Cione di Bello", which in turn extended "as far as the area of the Badia; and, through the houses and the area of the Badia, near to the bell tower as far as the street of the Palazzo del Comune...". This street corresponds, for the most part at least, to via de' Cimatori.

---

[36] From V. Imbriani we have the boundaries of these buildings: « unius domus posite in dicto populo, cuia I via, a II Casini Cimatoris Johannis de Circhulis, a III habbatie Florentie, a IV dicti Cionis et Bellini eius nepotis, et alterius medie domus posite in dicto populo, a I via, a II Casini Cimatoris, a III dicte Habbatie, a IV dicti Cionis». V. Imbriani, *Studi Danteschi*, Sansoni, Florence 1891, pp. 171-174.

[37] This source, from the Badia Fiorentina (ASF), is forwarded by Barbi in *Recensione a Bortolan*, pp. 68-69 and is taken up by Piranesi, *Le case degli Alighieri*, cit., pp. 45-47, and others.

Via de' Magazzini all'incrocio con via de' Cimatori.

For this reason, Cione di Bello's house, flanked by this street, occupied an area on Via de' Magazzini, towards Via del Proconsolo. According to Anna Franchi, it is therefore possible that the houses of at least part of the Alighieri family, together with the church of San Martino (whose apse must have been a little to the left, and a little back from today's entrance), formed a single block of buildings enclosed between what is now Via Dante Alighieri, Via de' Cerchi, Via de' Cimatori and Via dei Magazzini.[38] Its courtyard would roughly correspond to the area of the today's "Supercinema", the bar in Piazza San Martino and some shops, including one selling typical Korean products.

In fact, Piranesi had later located Cione's house on the

---

[38] A. Franchi, *Le case degli Alighieri*, cit., p. 745.

other side of today's Via de' Magazzini, in the light of descriptions in a document dated 11 August 1301[39]

It is not easy to get a clear idea of the situation of this *insula* in the 14th century, and how the land on which fig trees have grown was connected to Cione's or Alighiero's properties. Re-reading the descriptions in the documents, it seems that Cione's house may have stood almost at the end of Via de' Magazzini, next to the new road, on the side of the square, close to and visible from the other Alighieri houses.

When and why did the Alighieri move to the other side of the square? Was it Bello who built a new house for his son? It is more than likely. At the same time, we could speculate that Cacciaguida's sons already had some right to an area in this courtyard.

Certainly the most important Alighieri for this research lived on the other side of the church of San Martino, next to the present Casa Museo. And we must assume that Dante himself was among them.

Barbi-Piattoli's research

In 1938, Michele Barbi and Renato Piattoli revisited the question of the location of Dante's actual house, with a completely different depth to that of the Commission's investigations and those that followed. The essay, published in the Studi Danteschi,[40] is based on the

---

[39] This is the actual order in which the street was opened, with a modification in the last tract. G. Piranesi, *Sulla ubicazione e orientazione delle case degli Alighieri in Firenze*, Florence 1905, 3-6.

[40] M. Barbi-R. Piattoli, *La Casa di Dante*, cit., pp. 5 e seg.

history of the buildings on what is now Via Santa Margherita and Via Dante Alighieri/ Via di San Martino. The method is to work backwards in time, rather than starting with Alighiero and his sons. Moreover, all the houses of the Insula are taken into account, without immediately concentrating on those directly related to the Alighieri. The scope will be extended to include new data and possibilities.

The "Casa della Stufa" and the Mardoli workshop

After analysing the houses on the corner of the two streets (which coincides with the southern side of the museum), the researchers reconstruct, as far as possible, the history of ownership of the buildings, which belonged to the Arte della Lana (Wool Guild), the nearby Badia, the Monastery of San Miniato and some families, as well as inhabited by various tenants.

The so-called "Casa della Stufa" (internally connected to the Campani property mentioned in the 1865 Report) and other adjoining units can now be identified with certainty.[41] These often appear to be separated, but in fact they were connected in a large building complex, with an entrance in via Santa Margherita, which also had a workshop in via San Martino, bypassing the corner sections (later the property of the Arte della Lana); while on the other (northern) side the Donati properties expanded.

Going back in time, in the 15th and 14th centuries,

---

[41] Ibid., cit., p. 13.

members of the Cederni, Vecchietti, Cavalcanti and Biliotti families, and therefore of the Mardoli family, lived in this complex or in parts of it. These properties, previously fragmented, were reunited in Lapo di Niccolò Biliotti through inheritances and purchas. [42] An important detail is hidden among these inheritances.

The houses of Cione and Bellincione

The "contact" with the Alighieri came about thanks to a deed of sale from Monna Lippa, widow of Mardoli, to Lapo di Niccolò Biliotti in 1338. The deed mentions three neighbouring properties, one of which corresponds to the house of the Stufa, another to a fondaco later identified as the so-called "Stufa grande" and the third to a workshop place in via di San Martino. [43]

For the latter, on the "fourth side", the property of Cionis Brunetti, Dante's cousin, is mentioned. The building owned by Cione is thus identified by Barbi-Piattoli as a part of the existing houses in what is now Via Dante Alighieri. This property is mentioned in a cadastral table of 1610, related to a legal dispute, in which it seems to be the property of a certain Anton Galilei. [44]

It was already known that a house belonging to Cione di Brunetto is mentioned in another document of 1323 (in which it is ceded to Niccola di Giovanni da Vascappo), and that a Nicola dei Donati «vel Petrus

---

[42] M. Barbi-R. Piattoli, *La Casa di Dante*, cit., pp. 22-26.

[43] Ibid., pp. 26-27.

[44] Ibid., tav. 1.

Dantis Allegerii'»[45] appeared among the neighbours.

But even in the Libro del Danno of 1269, in which Geri's house appears «aliquantulum destructam», a house belonging to Bellincione di Alighiero is mentioned, still on the "fourth side".[46] In fact, the sons of the first Alighiero, Bello (Geri's father) and Bellincione, are said to have lived in neighbouring houses, inheriting their father's property, which was then further subdivided.[47] The house of Cione di Brunetto was part of the original house of Bellincione.

Hence the image of two Alighieri houses, once united and then divided, corresponding to the buildings facing the Torre della Castagna and Piazza San Martino. In this place, next to the old Mardoli workshop, would have been the house of Dante's grandfather.[48]

---

[45] M. Barbi-R. Piattoli, *La Casa di Dante*, cit., p. 30; and already M. Barbi in *Bullettino della Società Dantesca*, v. XII, 1905, pp. 316-320. The document appears in E. Casanova-R. Davidsohn, *Nuovi documenti della famiglia di Dante*, in *Bullettino della Società Dantesca*, v. VII, 1898, p. 98.

[46] M. Barbi-R. Piattoli, *La Casa di Dante*, cit., p.30.

[47] Barbi's summary of the possible divisions of the family houses is picturesque and illustrative: "Just as Bello lived with his sons, so Bellincione lived with his descendants. How the house was divided between the two brothers, and then between their sons, is impossible to determine today (...) some neighbours must have been common to the various parts of the house, even if it was not the case that one branch had rooms in the same position as the other, on different floors. Naturally, as the number of children grew, the house had to be adapted to their needs, and those who died, like Geri, or left to find more comfort, like his brother Cione, had to give up their place to the others". *Recensione a Bortolan*, p. 68.

[48] For more on these similarities, especially in relation to property boundaries and ownership, see M. Barbi-R. Piattoli, *La Casa di Dante*, cit., pp. 30-31.

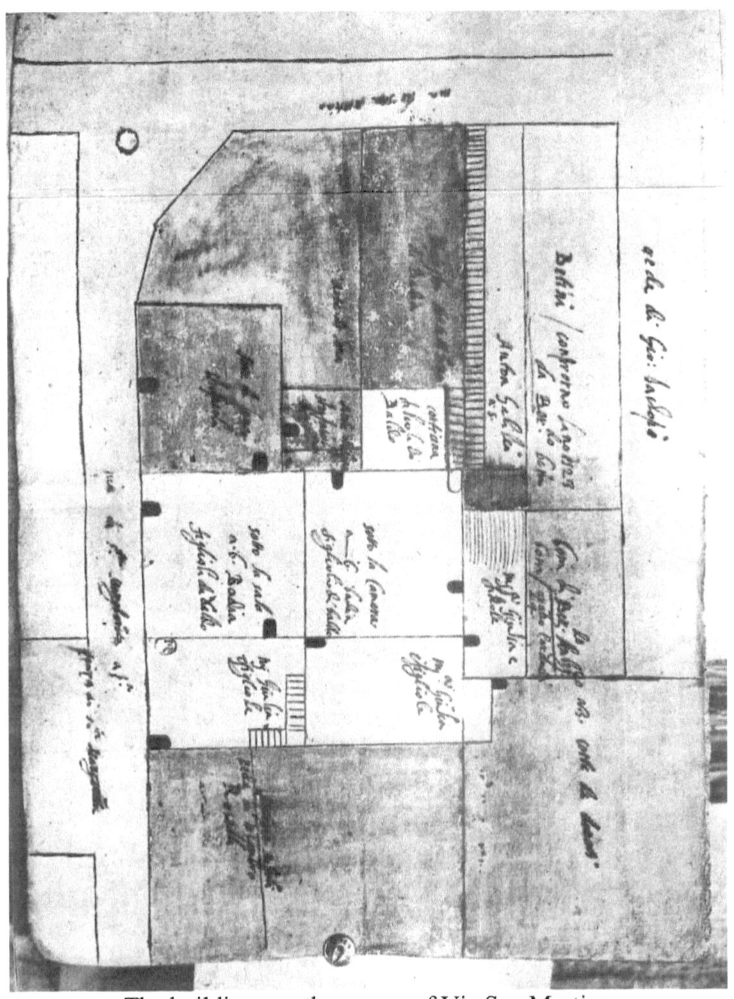

The buildings on the corner of Via San Martino
and Via Santa Margherita in a cadastral table of 1610
(from M. Barbi-R. Piattoli, 1938)

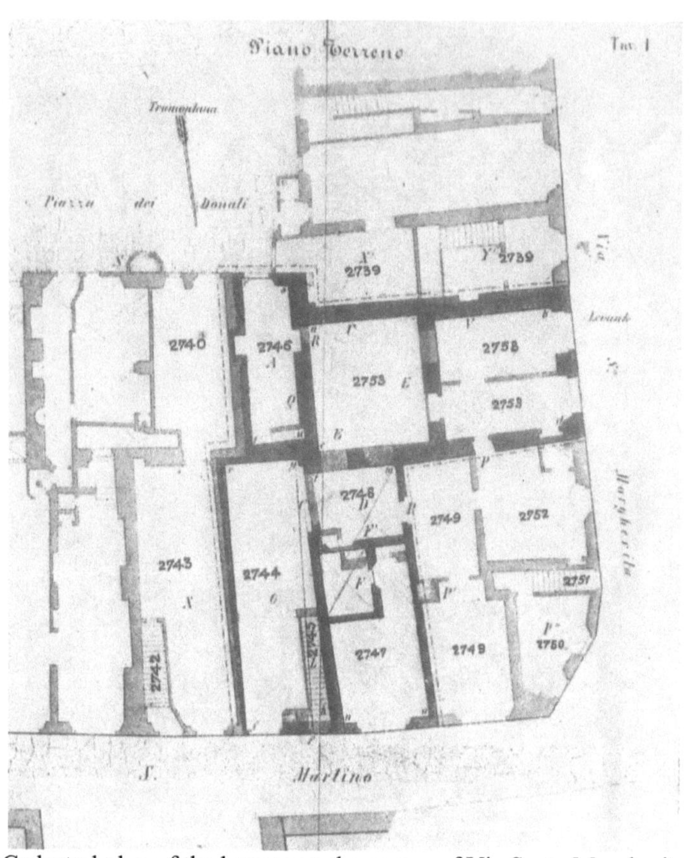

Cadastral plan of the houses on the corner of Via Santa Margherita
and Via San Martino (from the 1865 Report)

Where was he born, and where did he live?

Barbi-Piattoli question the distinction between the
house where Dante lived and the house where he was
born. Since these walls may still exist, it is probable that
the house where he was born was the same as that of
Bellincione, where Alighiero II lived, but which also
belonged to his brother Brunetto. Thus, Dante, who was

Bellincione's nephew, would have obtained the right to live in the neighbouring house of Geri.

This would have happened, according to Barbi-Piattoli,[49] because after Geri's death,[50] murdered by a Sacchetti, the western part of the house remained empty, while Cione di Bello (Geri's brother) and his son Lapo, as we have already seen, settled elsewhere in the neighbourhood.

Dante would have lived in the building where the Pennello restaurant is today, in a house that was also owned by Francesco. But the Poet would have been born in the building at number 2, in front of the Torre della Castagna.

The division of the family house

Let us return to the aforementioned deed of 16 May 1332, which testifies to the redemption by Dante's sons, Pietro and Iacopo of the alienated part of the Poet's supposed house, now shared with their uncle Francesco.

The adjacency with the Mardoli properties is clear, even if we find significant changes in the boundary features compared to previous documents.[51] The coincidence between this house and that of Geri, and its actual location in Via San Martino, were not definitively clarified until the Barbi-Piattoli study of 1938. At the

---

[49] M. Barbi-R. Piattoli, *La Casa di Dante*, cit., pp. 31-32.

[50] It occurred after 1276, when he was still alive, accused of brawling and beatings, in a trial in the city of Prato.

[51] With the appearance of the Cocchi and fractionations of the Donati. M. Barbi-R. Piattoli, La Casa di Dante, cit, p. 34.

turn of the century, Giorgio Piranesi expressed strong doubts, analysing the ambiguities of the context.[52] He also argued that the identification was based on the questionable tradition transmitted by Bruni and the existence of a Museum.[53]

It seems that the house in question had been saved from demolition by Dante's brother, perhaps thanks to a fictitious sale, with a ransom condition that would later allow Pietro and Iacopo to recover it from the hands of Gemma's nephew, Niccolò. This is how Barbi explains the «vel Petrus» in the document of 1323, further confirming the location of this part of the old family home,[54] while Piranesi, on the contrary, argued that it could be a completely different property.[55]

Returning to the 1332 document, we can identify the 'heredum Berti de Mardolis', who appear on the 'fourth side', with Niccolò Biliotti and others with rights to the houses all around. According to Barbi-Piattoli, the house still referred to in 1338 as "di Cione di Brunetto", had not been inhabited by him for some time, but was defined as such, referring to the old owner, to distinguish it from the homogeneity of the properties all around.[56] This would explain its absence in the 1332 document.

After regaining possession of part of the house where the Poet probably lived, Pietro and Iacopo had another

---

[52] G. Piranesi, *Autodifesa*, pp. 294-298, cfr. M. Barbi in *Bullettino della Società Dantesca*, v. XII, 1905, pp. 316-320.

[53] G. Piranesi, *Autodifesa*, p. 298.

[54] Giˆ in *Bullettino della Società Dantesca*, v. XII, 1905, p. 320.

[55] G. Piranesi, *Autodifesa*, p. 298.

[56] M. Barbi-R. Piattoli, *La Casa di Dante*, cit., pp. 34- 35.

dispute, which was settled in 1341,[57] After that, the property belongs to Peter alone. to Pietro alone. He left it in his will to the company of Orsanmichele.

The two halves were to be reunited in 1365 (one, probably returned to Francesco, passed to a Lupicini), when the entire estate came into the possession of Matteo Arrighi.[58]

The other houses of the Alighieri

The hypotheses and certainties about the houses of Geri and Bellincione, Cione di Brunetto and Pietro di Dante, however, allow us to investigate another house inhabited by the Alihghieri family, further away from the House Museum. There, on the other side of Piazza San Martino, lived the other Cione (son of Bello and therefore cousin of Dante's father) and his son Lapo, with whom Dante undoubtedly had a relationship.

While the obscure "question of the fig tree" is almost forgotten, the document of 1297 (in which the street coincides with today's Via de' Cimatori) is the subject of new criticism among scholars.

---

[57] Ibid., p. 35.

[58] Ibid., p. 36. The Arrighi were also the owners of the adjacent house, thanks to the will of Marco del fu Zebedeo, which was notarised with the promise to build a chapel in San Miniato al Monte. The chaplain himself was then endowed with property in San Martino, so much so that a house belonging to San Minitato appears in the documents, the location of which caused further controversy. Ibid., pp. 37-39 cfr. G. Piranesi, *Le case alighieri*, cit., pp. 27-30, e *Autodifesa*, pp. 294 e seg.

Via de' Cimatori seen from the corner with Via de' Magazzini

In his text of 1905, Piranesi had collected the above source, which Barbi had already mentioned in a previous article.[59]

But according to Piranesi in this case Barbi had not added "any special consideration of the houses of the

---

[59] *Recensione a Bortolan*, p. 68, cf. G. Piranesi, *Le case degli Alighieri*, cit. p. 45. This happened many times before the publication of Barbi-Piattoli's definitive research in 1938.

Alighieri"[60] and, moreover, he had made "one of his usual lyrical flights" («uno de' soliti voli lirici»), claiming that Cione and Lapo had emigrated from via San Martino "for greater comfort" («per loro maggior agio»).[61]

Piranesi perhaps makes the mistake of treating Barbi with a certain haughtiness – a typical behaviour of many scolars of the time. Barbi argues that a document from 1295, edited by Vittorio Imbriani in his *Studi Danteschi*,[62] had already deduced the residence of Cione, Geri's son, elsewhere from the buildings of Bellincione and Geri himself.[63] The latter figure had also been studied by Domenico Bortolan, whose errors of interpretation Barbi had pointed out.

The researchers exchanged a few jabs.[64] Some replies from Barbi and a "self-defence" from Piranesi, on the basis of another document (dated 1301)[65] that would only allow the houses of Cione, Lapo and Bellino to be even better located.

The matter died down by 1906, with no further reply from Barbi who laconically left «unanswered»[66] the long defence of Piranesi published in minute type in the last pages of the Bullettino.

---

[60] G. Piranesi, *Le case degli Alighieri*, cit., p. 45.

[61] It reads precisely «a trovare più agio» in Barbi, *Recensione a Bortolan*, p. 68.

[62] V. Imbriani, *Studi Danteschi*, cit., p. 171-174. This is the well-known ransom of two portions of the building belonging to Lapo, previously condemned for the assault on the Commune.

[63] M. Barbi-R. Piattoli, *La Casa di Dante*, cit., p. 32.

[64] During published exchanges of views in the *Bullettino della Società Dantesca*, v. XII, 1905, pp. 313-330 e v. XIII, 1906, pp. 293-298 (the *Autodifesa*).

[65] G. Piranesi, *Sulla ubicazione e orientazione delle case degli Alighieri in Firenze*, Firenze 1905, pp. 3-6.

[66] M. Barbi-R. Piattoli, *La Casa di Dante*, cit., p. 32.

Barbi would later speak of Piranesi as "a mind unaccustomed to the subtleties of criticism".[67]

Since then, Piranesi's observations have been considered obsolete and are not even mentioned in more recent publications. However, in addition to questioning the inaccuracies of the first Report, we believe that we owe to this researcher part of the spark that activated the research that led to the best possible solution, the one revealed by Barbi-Piattoli.

Let us not forget that Piranesi, whose writings had a certain resonance, was the first to argue that Dante's houses might not have existed, or that they might have been located elsewhere. This obviously triggered a reaction in terms of research, to the point of a better understanding of the context.

Piranesi's research is at the origin of the "trend" according to which it is still possible to read in Wikipedia that the Alighieri's houses were "actually (...) in Via de' Magazzini". Be that as it may, it prompts us to focus more on this context and to investigate the vicissitudes of Dante's relatives who lived there.

We believe that the two Alighieri sites, of which the southern one (belonging to the Di Bello family) may still be partially explored, can be considered as a single system. The barycenter of this system would coincide with the fig tree that grew in a garden square that the Alighieri used in ancient times almost as their courtyard, disputing with the clerics who would have preferred to fence it off or even build new buildings there.[68]

---

[67] M. Barbi-R. Piattoli, *La Casa di Dante*, cit., p. 32.

[68] There is evidence of a court case between 1276 and 1277 in which a

Via de' Magazzini buildings facing Via de' Cimatori

group of local people, on the one hand, and the monks of the Badia and the rector of San Martino, on the other, opposed the construction of buildings around the church, that is to say in the present square. In this context, it is worth remembering a specific statement by Bello Alighieri that he had placed stones on this land, probably in anticipation of the extension of the buildings further south. For these and other facts about Bello and Cione, see in particular M. Barbi, *Cenni di M. Bello Alighieri* in *Studi Danteschi*, v. I, 1920, pp. 132-136.

In the preceding pages we have attempted to offer a synthesis of the complex research that has occupied the minds of scholars of great depth, engaged in the analysis of specific, albeit very close, places. Much more has been written and done since then, but for some reasons our interest has focused on that remote yet significant phase.

Many decades later, looking back on that period and trying to read "between the lines" of those writings, it seems to us that the knot of greatest interest continues to be the question of the location of ancient buildings. Why, in some cases, do certain Florentines (scholars and others) welcome the idea that Dante might be sought elsewhere than where we usually "place" him?

We do not believe that the answer to this question lies in the fact that Florence had a "conflictual relationship" with Dante, who was exiled a good seven hundred years ago. Nor, knowing the Florentines, do we believe that they are trying to "dematerialise" the royal house in order to rediscover the philosophical purity of Dante's contribution. Rather, we should ask ourselves how the relationship between a Dantean idealism, perhaps sometimes divorced from reality, and a still fiery spirituality has developed in the city: that of a "Dante" that Papini would have liked to see more "alive".[69]

---

[69] G. Papini, *Dante vivo*, LEF, Florence 1933. The discussion on "anti-Dantismo" and the diatribe between "dantisti" and "dantomani" characterised the years in which research on Dante's House also took place, with episodes in the same journals where the authors already mentioned appeared. See for example E. G. Parodi, *Moderno Antidantismo*, in *Bullettino della Società Dantesca*, v.

The answer to this question is probably beyond us. However, we can observe how such specific studies, presented in a complex chronology and rarely supported by synthesis work and sharing, has made the problem of the house's location inaccessible to non-experts. A kind of "historiographical curtain" has implicitly been created, which discourages anyone from the challenge of in-depth study, and perhaps makes it more difficult to de-escalate the problems mentioned above.

Be that as it may, the high probability that Dante's house was located where the Pennello restaurant is today has been confirmed by various writers[70] who have regularly returned to the subject in articles published in guides, books, bulletins and magazines, so much so that the managers of the same restaurant keep a framed clipping in the dining room.

Piero Bargellini is one of these authors. The mayor and writer, in his *Vita di Dante* (1964), first describes a "cradle" of Dante, "rocking on hot days in the shade of this tree"[71] near the apse of San Martino, and then concludes that not far away, "beyond the road that led to the house of Sacchetti, squeezed between the tower of the Giuochi and the Donati, was the Alighieri's house".[72]

XIII, 1906, pp. 128 ff.

70 On the heterogeneity of opinions, we recall M. Dezzi Bardeschi, Il *Monumento e il suo doppio*, Alinari, Firenze 1981, p. 47, and E. Giani, who in 2015, during a conference at the Circolo degli Artisti, spoke of the "real location" of the Sommo Poet's birthplace. In these circumstances, the room (above the Pennello restaurant) where Dante could have been born was indicated (*La Nazione,* 20 May 2015).

71 Piero Bargellini, *Vita di Dante*, Vallecchi, Firenze 1964, p. 15.

72 Ibidem.

In this fortunate case of synthesis, the author maintains an openness to the dimension of the Rione while locating the dwellings along via San Martino. He also offers us confirmation of the impression that the "sphere" of research on Dante's house could find its centre in the fateful fig tree, now imbued with secular sacredness.

And who knows if Dante himself, testifying to the purer side of Florentine life, had not imagined this fig tree when he used the image in Canto XV (verse 66) of the Inferno. In fact, we have no certainty, as Bargellini himself points out, that the plant was finally uprooted in Alighiero's time.

A painting by Raffaello Sorbi in S. Margherita

In 2013, the documentary film "Fiorendipità" (title is a play on words between "serendipity" and "florentinity") attempted a direct confrontation with the current daily life of the Rione, in search of its "soul".[73]

The shopkeepers and some of the passers-by interviewed testify to a certain disillusionment with the Dantean tradition. Florentines, too, are said to be scarce in these streets, and the houses are inhabited mainly by tourists and foreigners.[74]

Those who work at Pennello's confirm the identity between the restaurant and the "real home of Dante", but someone raises the hypothesis that the Alighieri also lived in the block now occupied by the Supercinema, which seems to have an exit on Piazza San Martino.

We then arrived at the Korean goods shop, on the corner of Via dei Magazini/ Via de' Cimatori, and put our questions to the owner. She led us to No. 2 Via Alighieri, indicating Dante's birthplace near the place where Cione di Brunetto and Bellincione lived.

Of all the shopkeepers in the area, the Korean-Florentine seems to be the one with the clearest idea of the location of the house.

---

[73] *Fiorendipità, storia e anima del Rione di Dante*, di L. Pecchioni, Press & Archeos, 2013. The documentary, from which the text you are reading is largely taken, was in turn inspired by an earlier pamphlet containing some observations by E. Pecchioni, *Piccola guida al Rione dantesco*, self-published, Florence 2012) centred mainly on Piranesi-Franchi's hypothesis.

[74] The documentary contains some curious emotional notes: "It does not flow. It does not stream. It is not refreshed...". See documentary *Fiorendipità*, cit., 2013.

Inconsistency and coexistence

In the Dantesque district, there are undoubtedly some disturbing or misleading presences.[75] The coexistence of old citizenship and elements of novelty is not a simple problem and is, in fact, as old as mankind. It helps us to think that such a problem also existed in the time of the Poet.

Dante himself, under certain circumstances, seems to understand that in the city of Florence there is a problem of confrontation with the passage of time and with more modern needs. The city, yesterday as well as today, is expanding, mixing with new people. On the one hand, Dante seems to lean towards a vision of integration... only to return as a conservative.[76]

These questions seem to be alive in the mind of someone who lived Florentine life in a profound and passionate way. We see the continuity of a questioning that is sometimes modelled on the complex relationship between the city and the exiled Poet.

From Florence to Fiesole

On 27 January 1302, the sentence pronounced against the White Guelphs convicts sounded more or less like this: "... if the fine is not paid within three days of the sentence, the property of the insolvent shall be published, plundered and disposed of, and so spoiled and unused

---

[75] Please note that the documentary was produced in 2013.

[76] See the observations of L. Conti Lapi interviewed in the documentary *Fiorendipità*, cit.

shall remain with the Comune".[77] It is known that Dante had many debts, and it seems unlikely that the family could withstand this wrath. Many of the family moved away from the city although, just as likely, as we have seen, the houses were not or only partially destroyed.

San Miniato a Pagnolle (Pontassieve, FI)

Francesco Alighieri somehow managed to retain the rights to part of the house in via San Martino, which he was to share with his nephews. Later, in 1343, Jacopo Alighieri tried to recover some family properties outside Florence: a possessione "cum vinea, et cum domibus super ea, combustis et non combustis, posita in populo S. Miniatis de Pagnola",[78] and also four other plots of land in Pagnolle, not far from Fiesole.

These places, close to the Fiesole "rock", although

---

[77] Anna Franchi, *Le case degli Alighieri*, cit., p. 743.

[78] G. Piranesi, *Le case degli Alighieri*, cit., p. 52.

"without sweet figs",[79] are ideally connected to Dante's neighbourhood. And some have imagined that Dante spent some of his summer holidays here, before his exile. The Alighieri cottage is identified with the house of Radola (or Le Radole), originally called *Radere*,[80] where a beautiful tower still stands. Nearby is the Montecchi farmhouse, owned by the Portinari family: is it possible that Dante and Beatrice met in Pagnolle?

We do not know if any of the refugee family lived in these places: it seems that the enemies, in their eagerness to destroy and take possession, even went beyond Fiesole to «combustere» (set fire) to the houses of the Guelph Bianco.

But let us return to Florence.

If, as we said at the beginning of our research, we had really arrived in the Dante district at dawn in order to perceive some kind of essence, we would now have reached the middle of the day, after a long and dutiful interrogation about the Alighieri houses.

During the peak hours, the tourists are more numerous, walking in groups through the streets. The phenomenon of the attraction of Dante never ceases and has certain characteristics: after a chat in front of the house and the bust of Rivalta (where we have immersed ourselves in the research of the "native walls"), everyone

---

[79] In INFERNO, XV, 61-74, Dante condemns that "malignant people" of Fiesole (rough and harsh like the "boulder" from which it comes), in the midst of which it is «it is not fitting that sweet figs bear fruit».

[80] U. Dorini, *Ancora dei beni rurali confiscati a Dante - le divise fatte dai figliuoli Pietro e Iacopo nel 1341 e 1347*, in *Bullettino della Societ^ Dantesca*, vol. XIII, 1906, pp. 58.

or almost everyone goes to the little church known as Dante's, or Santa Margherita dei Cerchi.

Afterwards, or as an alternative, a spontaneous visit to the Oratory of San Martino, which is usually open during the first part of the day.

Dante's Churches

Santa Margherita dei Cerchi

The church of Santa Margherita, or "Dante's Church", first mentioned in 1032, was under the patronage of Cerchi, Adimari and Donati from 1353 and of Cerchi alone from the 17th century. Members of the Portinari family are buried here. The church is dedicated to St. Margaret of Antioch, testimony to the close relationship between the Florentine families and the early Christian martyrs: those whose stories take place in the Holy Land. One thinks, above all, of Saint Reparata.

Until the middle of the twentieth century, the small church was in a state of neglect and decay. Then, thanks to the efforts of its rector Luigi Stefani, it was completely restored and returned to the Florentines. From the passionate testimonies of this priest[81] we learn some denunciations of the forgetfulness to which Dante was subjected, but also interesting notes on the titular saint.

Margaret has always been regarded as the protector of pregnant women. In a well-known passage of her legend, the saint, swallowed by a dragon, manages to free herself by cutting open her belly with the sign of the cross. This episode is an exceptional case of symbolic narration, capable of linking the image of Margaret to the successful completion of childbirth in an exuberant but appropriate

---

[81] L. Stefani, *Dante e la sua Chiesa*, Quaderni de «Lo Sprone», Firenze 1979.

Image of St. Margaret and her church visible in the 15th century.
Rustici Codex (from L. Stefani, cit.)

way. The negative value associated with the figure of the dragon and the descent/return from the underworld to which it refers is not to be overlooked.

It is certain that the church was the object of particular devotion by the women of this part of the city, and therefore of the Quartiere itself, who sought the intercession of the saint in the dramatic and sometimes fatal moments of pregnancy.

Inside we find an altarpiece painted by Neri di Bicci, which is entirely female: Mary appears between Saint Lucy, Saint Margaret, Saint Agnes and Saint Catherine of Alexandria. Lucia is a name that recurs in Dante's hagiographic interests and appears several times in the Commedia.

Pregnant matriarchal values seem to permeate the church of Santa Margherita: in it can be seen a cast of the tomb of Monna Tessa, who worked for many years for the Portinari family and who inspired Folco, Beatrice's father, to found the hospital of Santa Maria Nuova. On the other side of the nave there is a "tombstone" of Beatrice Portinari.

For some years now, next to this plaque, there has been a basket for written prayers addressed to Beatrice, who has been chosen as a mediator, a "saint", a vehicle for the prayers of lovers. In short, this church is a small temple in which the figure of the woman is pleasantly celebrated.

Beatrice, who was married to Simone de' Bardi, was almost certainly buried in the Bardi Chapel of Santa Croce, while her father Folco was buried here in the church in what is now the Dante's Neighborhood.

The church of Santa Margherita de' Cerchi

Among the many, perhaps too many,[82] paintings in the church is a fine painting by Raffaello Sorbi, which depicts a medieval wedding with Macchiaioli wit. The Poet is seen walking away from the wall in his typical red dress: perhaps it is Beatrice and her Bardi who have

---

[82] With this remark, contained in the text of the documentary *Fiorendipità* (cit.), we referred to an exhibition of contemporary paintings that had been in the church for a long time.

married?

Another religious and gastronomic curiosity: the church of Santa Margherita is the seat of the Venerable Compagnia dei Quochi, whose patron saint is San Pasquale di Baylon, inventor of zabaglione and patron saint of cooks.

Lintel of the entrance portal of Santa Margherita de' Cerchi

The cast of Mona Tessa's funerary bas-relief

San Martino al Vescovo

Having visited, as far as we were able and allowed, the Dantean sites par excellence, let us move on to nearby Piazza San Martino, where, as we have seen, history once again prevails over tradition and the presence of the Alighieri is equally sensitive.

Here we find, immediately to the left, the Torre della Castagna. Opposite the entrance to the tower, on the other side of the square, is the Oratory of San Martino del Vescovo, whose dedication dates back to 986. The ancient church was probably the parish church of the Alighieri and Donati families, who were its patrons. The ancient church was probably the parish church of the Alighieri and Donati families, who were its patrons. The Romanesque building had very different features from the present one and was larger, stretching from Piazza San

Entrance to the Oratory of San Martino

Interior of the Oratory of San Martino

One of the episodes from the frescoes on the life of St Martin, inside
the Oratory of San Martino

of the ancient portal can be seen. The ancient right side nave, if its existence can be proven, would today be occupied by some of the rooms of the Super Cinema.

The façade therefore faced west and the church was oriented in the traditional way, with the apse facing the sunrise. But in this case, in Alighiero's time, the mystical rays were filtered by the leaves of the fig trees... if not blocked by the surrounding buildings.

In the late Middle Ages, the parish was definitively suppressed due to the ecclesiastical reorganisation of the city, which had greatly increased in population.

In 1441 San Martino became the seat of the Compagnia dei Dodici Buonuomini, founded by San Antonino Pierozzi, Bishop of Florence, for the secret relief of fallen noble families, the so-called "poveri vergognosi" (shameful poor).

It seems that the society is still going strong. So if someone in trouble thought of lighting a candle in front of the entrance to the oratory, a member of the confraternity would have to come forward to help. Minimum requirement: to be born in the territory of the Commune of Florence ...

Inside the Oratory there is a series of ten frescoes with stories of Saint Martin and representations of the works of mercy, attributed to Francesco d'Antonio, of great interest for the history of 15th century Florentine costume. It is as if we were seeing the inhabitants of the old town, members of historical dynasties, in the midst of their daily lives. Cerchi, Donati, Sacchetti, Alighieri ...

Presumed remains of the entrance portal of the first church of San Martino, visible in the Canto della "Quarconia". This curious toponym is said to derive from the Latin locution *quare coniam* (translatable as "for what reason why") used in sentences of condemnation; or perhaps from the presence of a craftsman who habitually pronounced these words, reciting verses from *Psalm 92*.

The Badia Fiorentina, located in front of the Bargello, along the road that, according to the 1297 source transmitted by Barbi,[83] led from the Palazzo Municipale to Dante's district, is also one of the places that Dante certainly frequented.

The Benedictine church, founded in 979 by Countess Willa, mother of Ugo Marquis of Tuscany († 1001), played an important role in the political life of the city from the time of the Marquisate to that of the first republican priors who settled there. In 1285 it was enlarged in the Cistercian style. At that time it had an Arnolfoesque façade facing west, which is still partially visible from the courtyard of the former Magistrate's Court in Piazza di San Martino. In the 17th century it was radically rebuilt in neoclassical style.

Inside there are precious works by Bernardo Rossellino and Mino da Fiesole. We find the tomb of Count Ugo Marquis of Tuscany (created by Mino da Fiesole) in front of which celebrations have been held for over a thousand years on the anniversary of his death (21 December).

The Madonna Appearing to St. Bernard by Filippino Lippi, one of the most important masterpieces of 15th century Florentine art, comes from the vanished monastery of Santa Maria di Santo Sepolcro alle Campora, whose property was inherited by the Benedictine monks of the Badia.

The abbey has been famous for centuries for its

---

[83] *Recensione a Bortolan*, p. 68.

collection of relics, which have recently given rise to bizarre hypotheses.[84]

Interior of the Badia Fiorentina church

<hr>

[84] We refer to some hypotheses, almost fantastic, concerning the preservation in Florence of the relics of the last Grand Master of the Knights Templar; this would have been done by the Girolamini monks, whose definitive seat was Santa Maria delle Campora. See the documentary *Le ceneri di Jacques De Molay*, Mediaframe, Firenze 2013.

San Remigio

Between the Badia Fiorentina and the Arno, in a small square next to Via Vinegia, is the ancient church of San Remigio, where the Alighieri are said to have had a chapel.

The church was built in 1040 on the site of an ancient hostel that had been used since the 9th century to welcome French pilgrims on their way to Rome. The building was therefore very close to the city walls, as were the hostels. The cult of Saint Remigius is widespread in France, but this saint also had some important sanctuaries in Italy, although there are very few in Tuscany. One of them, in Fosdinovo, was visited by Dante.[85]

San Remigio took on its present appearance in 1350, when it was restored and enlarged. Families who had altars or chapels in the building participated economically: Alberti, Pepi, Bagnesi and Alighieri.[86] In fact, one of the chapels "belonged, it is said, to Dante Alighieri (...)". If we try to deepen the relationship between Alighieri and San Remigio, we discover the uncertainty of this tradition.

The enlargement of the building was made possible by the donation of a neighbouring house, with permission to build on it, by Gherardo Aldighieri in 1303.

---

[85] Dante had a special relationship with the Malaspina family, whose representative he was in 1306, during the Peace of Castelnuovo. Lunigiana was neutral to the disputes between Whites and Blacks and it is possible that the Poet settled there for a time.

[86] G. Formigli, *Guida per la città di Firenze e i suoi contorni*, Forni, Firenze 1849, p. 177. The information seems to come from G. Richa, *Notizie istoriche chelle chiese fiorentine*, cit., t. I, p. 259 («Finally we are in the chapel once belonging to Dante Alighieri, and then to the Gaddi family (...)».

Sinopia with tournament scene visible inside San Remigio

Gherardo's patronal chapel («the one on the left, looking at the high altar»[87]) was inherited in the 17th century by Niccolò Gaddi. The latter, «to honour the memory of Dante, ordered to Jacopo Chimenti ("L'Empoli") a painting of the Immaculate Conception (now lost), [88] inspired by the verses of the Divine Comedy: "Here is the rose in which the divine Word / became flesh, and here are the lilies / by whose perfume the good way was taken».[89]

Doubts about the connection between the notary Gherardo Aldighieri and the Alighieri who lived in San Martino at the same time had already been expressed by Pelli, who attributed them to different lineages.[90] But the same scholar recalls the similarity of the surnames of many Florentine families, which does not exclude the possibility of a distant common ancestry that tradition may have preserved. Moreover, the Allighieri di San

---

[87] P. Bargellini-E. Guarnieri, *Le strade di Firenze*, Bonechi, Firenze 1978, v. III, p. 212.

[88] It is described G. Richa, *Notizie istoriche chelle chiese fiorentine, cit.*, p. 259.

[89] P. Bargellini-E. Guarnieri, *Le strade di Firenze*, cit., v. III, p. 212, cfr. PARADISO, XX, 73-75.

[90] G. B. Pelli, *Memorie per servire alla vita di Dante Alighieri ed alla storia della sua famiglia*, Piatti, Firenze 1823, pp. 22-23.

Martino, as they are called in Boccaccio, are mentioned in documents with many variations. Going back to the distant past, the existence of these onomastic correspondences could once again lead us to other places (and further east) than the houses in Via San Martino.

The church of San Remigio has preserved its late medieval layout, with its characteristic gabled roof and octagonal columns, apart from limited Baroque interventions and the usual 20th century restorations.

The interior surprises with some references that could be described as "Courtly", such as a hunting scene, the sinopia of a fresco of a knightly tournament, the baptism of the Merovingian king Clovis and Saint Remigius himself. One breathes a European atmosphere that is not at odds with Dante's imagery (think of Dante's journey to France, which many have hypothesised).

San Remigio was also very close to the Peruzzi residence: the square named after them is just a few steps behind the church. The Peruzz family were constantly trading with the French and had relations with the Hierosolymitan and Templar orders, which were the most widespread in France. On the vaults of the Alighieri chapel in San Remigio, a Maltese cross can capture the imagination of the "last-minute templars".

The façade of the church of San Remigio, in the square
of the same name

TOWER HOUSES, REVENGE AND SCANDALS

The public tower of the Castagna

The Torre della Castagna is a rather peculiar case of a "tower house", not related to historical families, for the public and institutional function it still fulfils.

Quadrangular and slender, it belonged to the Benedictines and was erected to defend the Florentine Abbey, to which it was donated by Conrad II. From 1282, with the abbot's permission and protection, the high magistrates of the priors and the arts took refuge there "so that they would not have to fear the threats of the powerful", writes Dino Compagni. It seems that the name of the tower comes from the chestnuts (*castagne*) that the priors used to vote with, putting them in a sack, before they were replaced by coloured balls.

If the tower still has a good height, it is because its public function spared it from the numerous family feuds. After the suppression of the monastery, it passed to the Municipality of Florence and was restored in 1920 on the occasion of the celebrations of Dante's sesquicentennial. Before these interventions, some of the windows and, in particular, the large entrance facing Piazza San Martino, had been bricked up.

Today it is the seat of the Garibaldini National Association, which has set up a small museum.

The entrance to the Torre della Castagna on Piazza San Martino

The Torre della Castagna seen from Via Dante Alighieri

Coming from San Martino along via de' Magazzini and arriving at the corner of via Condotta, we find the buildings coinciding with the houses of the Sacchetti, an ancient family that often opposed the Alighieri. The surviving tower, located in the old hamlet of Sant'Apollinare, is in ashlar stone up to the first floor, with windows that were badly obscured and dishevelled in the 19th century; above it is in filaretto, while the upper part is plastered.

The family is one of the oldest in the city. Originally from Fiesole, they moved to Florence after the destruction of Fiesole (in 1125) and held important positions: no less than thirty-two priors and eight gonfaloni. The Sacchetti also had a poet: Franco Sacchetti, novelist and podestà in various places in Tuscany and Emilia.

The Sacchetti were zealous defenders of the "true faith", being part of those fanatical bands that slaughtered many Patarine heretics. This could also explain their antipathy towards the Alighieri family, with its White and pro-imperial tradition.

The fates of the Alighieri and the Sacchetti crossed with the episode of the murder of Geri di Bello Alighieri, which took place around 1280, in the context of the conflicts between the political factions. Dante's sons tell us about it, referring to a «brodaio» ("broth cookman") of the opposing family.[91]

---

[91] In his *Commento*, Pietro di Dante states: «... Occiso olim per quemdam Brodarium de Sacchettis de Florentia». M. Barbi points out that the name Brodaio appears several times in the family tree of the Sacchetti family. Pietro

In revenge, a son of Cione (Geri's brother) killed a Sacchetti "in the doorway of his house". Perhaps the two men had been living too close for some time, and this added to the escalation.[92]

The palace corresponding to the tower house of the Sacchetti

then claims that the «nepotes dicti Geri in eius ultione quemdam de dictis Sacchettis occiderunt». *Recensione a Bortolan*, cit., p. 70.

[92] Anna Franchi, *Le case degli Alighieri*, cit., p. 746.

As we have seen, the first episode is crucial for hypotheses about Dante's real residence. According to Barbi, the Poet would have settled in Geri's house in via San Martino, which had been left empty after the crime and because Cione had already moved elsewhere.[93]

Compared to other bloody family feuds that lasted for generations, the one between Alighieri and Sacchetti did not degenerate into an uncontrollable series of vendettas. In 1342, at the behest of Governor Gualtieri di Brienne, a peace treaty was signed between the two families, putting an end to the matter once and for all.[94]

This was made possible by the fact that the Bello Alighieri branch, which had been directly involved in the bloody events, was now extinct or almost so.

Cerchi and Donati

The enmities between the historical families are essential to understand these neighbourhoods.

Adjacent to Via del Corso, but very close to the church and Dante's house, is Piazza dei Donati and the tower of the same name. The small square offers a splendid view of medieval Florence. A plaque commemorates Dante's memory of Corso Donati, a brave knight who, after siding with the Neri and later with the Ghibellines, was besieged in his fortress near San Pier Maggiore. Corso was forced to flee on horseback, pursued by the crowd.

---

[93] *Recensione a Bortolan*, cit., p. 68.

[94] V. Imbriani, *Illustrazioni al capitolo dantesco del Centiloquio*, Marghieri, Napoli 1880, p.16, cfr. *Recensione a Bortolan*, cit., p. 69.

He fell, became entangled in the stirrups and was captured and killed in the San Salvi area.

The Donati's worst enemies were the Cerchi, traditionally White, whose tower houses were incredibly close to those of their rivals. There is a small square dedicated to the Cerchi along via de' Cimatori, while the so-called Torre de' Cerchi stands between via de' Cerchi and via de' Cimatori.

The tower of the de' Cerchi family

The family, of the White Guelph tradition, bought the building from the Counts Guidi at the end of the 13th century, enlarging and fortifying it. The Cerchi probably had several towers, the remains of which can be seen along Via Cimatori, where there was also a loggia with arches that can still be seen today. The Cerchi's loggia is also remembered by Bargellini as the forerunner of the "natural loggias", the trees found elsewhere in the neighbourhood.[95]

The tower of the Donati family

---

[95] In reference to Alighiero's well-known fig tree. P. Bargellini, *Vita di Dante*, cit., p. 15.

After the exile of the Cerchi family in 1302, when Dante himself was exiled, the Torre de' Cerchi lived a rather quiet life, so much so that today we can see it in its almost original state.

Not everyone knows, but archaeology has confirmed it, that the Ghibelline and Guelph quarters were divided at the level of Piazza Signoria. Excavations carried out in the 1980s have allowed us to understand how this "division" was organised.

The Uberti Tower, on the Ghibelline side, was the stronghold of the district, flanked by the Palazzo della Signoria.

The Alley of Scandal

The history of 14th-century Florence seems to be centred on the dualism between the White Guelphs and the Black Guelphs, who coexisted in neighbouring blocks. There is one particularly representative site.

In 1350, the Florentine magistracy decided to build a street, now called "dello Scandalo" but once called "del Panico", in order to reduce the tensions between the rival families, in particular between the Cerchi and the Donati.

Much has changed in the area, but Vicolo dello Scandalo still exists.

It stretches for about 150 metres between Via Dante Alighieri and Via del Corso, winding its way through a series of corners before coming to an end. The ancient buildings that cling to it, throwing their arches and supports from one side to the other, have never covered the walkway, respecting the ancient ordinance.

Despite its important symbolic value, it is impossible not to notice that the alley has been a forgotten and degraded place for decades. Hence its inevitable recent closure, with two gates that until recently were simply left ajar. Now only residents and owners of properties with their backs to the alley have access to it.

Not a trace of tourists, then or now, although people from all over the world crowd into the small square of Dante's house. In this Alley, where ideas have sculpted the walls and pavements, tourists do not even know they can get there.

Glimpse of Scandal Alley

In a publication a few years ago, the street was associated with 'infernal omens'. The walls of the houses, dense with narrow windows and small tabernacles, the high roofs and the lack of sunlight, the feeling of claustrophobia and irreversibility that one feels when walking along it, are reminiscent of the ravines that led to underground entrances in many ancient legends. It is therefore possible to think of the beginning of Dante's Comedy, the entrance to the first circle of hell.[96]

An image of the Virgin Mary, placed above the entrance to the alley (from Via del Corso), seems to be there to ward off some kind of "danger". Perhaps the danger of crossing a line, with all the risks of "panic" that this entails. A separation from the Other in the broadest sense: another group, another creed...anyway an object of unconscious projection.

If our research had begun at dawn on a summer's day, as it did during the shooting of the documentary movie "Fiorendipità", we would now be well into the afternoon. In the "depths" of the Panic Alley, the light would hardly reach us. Even if the alley were still open, no one would be there, not even the vagabonds who used to sleep there late into the night. And immersed in the eerie solitude, we could imagine the dragon, torn apart by Saint Margaret, dragging itself here from the nearby church to die in its underworld...

Let's be clear, we're just being imaginative, because legends like this simply don't exist! But perhaps this is

---

[96] Bernardo Tavanti, *Le porte degli inferi in Toscana*, Press & Archeos, Firenze 2014, p. 87.

what is remarkable: in Dante's neighbourhood there are no traditions linked to the entrance to the Underworld.

Video frames from the Scandal Alley

LOOKING FOR THE GATE TO HELL?

One wonders how it is possible that here, where everything seems to refer to Dante and his Comedy, a place, a "door", a fountain, a well... has not been designated for a legend linked to the fateful "descent into hell". Or are we missing something?

Some of Dante's most acute connoisseurs will tell us that, in the Commedia, Florence is "already the Inferno". By showing the city of Dis, the Poet was alluding to his native city. In other words, we would already be 'inside' hell, or in the imaginary structure that can evoke it. We believe, however, that the absence of a legend worthy of mention and definable as such can raise some questions.

We could point out, for example, that in the history of myths the 'descent into the underworld' has always been a symbol of the beginning of an inner journey, of self-knowledge. So wouldn't the Florentines have identified Dante's district as a base from which to rediscover and recognise themselves? This would bring us back to what was said at the beginning of this book.

But let us leave open one possibility, however rarely practised.

"Sussi e Biribissi" is a famous novel set in Florence, written by the grandson of the author of Pinocchio, known as Collodi Nipote. When Sussi and Biribissi, two young boys, descend to the centre of the earth in search of new adventures - but above all of their inner selves - they find the ancient sewers, carved out of the medieval and even Roman city: "an ancient city, organised by others, but part of a logic that leads back to ourselves".[97]

Insofar as we can look for a link between the city of Dante's "dream" and the one contained in the Ancient Circle, we can say that even two little boys, in a fairy tale, objectively "bypassed the Poet" in the imaginary of an all-Florentine descent into hell!

In Florence, we notice the almost total absence of places directly linked to an imaginary Inferno. This is a curious fact, because when we leave the city, we find many places where Dante is said to have been inspired to write his Inferno: for example, the "Orrido di Botri" (near Pistoia), the "blazing grounds" of Pietramala, the "hell valleys" (near Arezzo), the numeros "infernacci"' and the "bulicami" (boiling pools) of Etruria, or many others. Then, many cities have legends about an infernal entrance, such as Lucca, Chiusi, Prato, Siena... just talking about Tuscanny.

Moreover, in the reinterpretation of Dante's imagery, the most important suggestions have come from outside, not from Florence. Just think of Dan Brown's novel, with its inferno and all its mysteries. Other traditions, such as that of the Sasso in Piazza del Duomo, or that of Beatrice - but these are "little pictures", rather than full-blown legends - were born or consolidated in the tourist era, generally levelling out in symbols. Sometimes the figure of Dante himself has been distorted, myths have been created, such as the funeral mask of Dante Alighieri, about which there are many doubts, but which certainly

---

[97] These are words of Mario Pagni, captured during an interview for the documentary *Fiorendipità*, cit.

appeals to an international audience.[98]

Recently, however, the city seems to have rediscovered the fascination of its underground passages, sometimes out of simple curiosity, with initiatives concerning the city's aqueduct or sewerage system, and sometimes in an esoteric sense, with fantasies about certain "Templar" tunnels.

In this sense, we already find allusions to a dark and subterranean Florence in a documentary by Massimo Becattini, who rediscovers the Roman city through a descent into the sewers.[99] At the beginning of the video, the shadows of Sussi and Biribissi appear, destined for another journey to the centre of the earth.

This curious episode leads us to playfully imagine the possibility of a connection between the Quartiere Dantesco and the underground of the "public waters" of Florence.

We could not help but do so... and, with a playful eye, examine the details of Dante's places; for example, the choreographic well at the side of Dante's house, now sealed by a metal plate.

The fountain is of recent construction, but if we go back in time, we find traces of a similar presence not far from the Alighieri buildings in via San Martino.[100]

Water, in its own way, was a protagonist in the medieval district, where we can imagine a spring of Santa

---

[98] Si veda E. Baccarini intervistato nel documentario *Fiorendipità*, cit.

[99] *La città dimenticata, storia archeologica della città di Firenze*, Film Documentari d'Arte, distr. Giunti, Firenze 1992.

[100] Also in the cadastral table of 1610, published by Barbi-Piattoli. But see, in the same text, another mention of the aforementioned well. M. Barbi-R. Piattoli, *La Casa di Dante*, cit., p. 66.

Margherita or a well of San Martino.

Moreover, in more recent times we have seen the existence of a house of the Stufa, or rather two: at least one of them is included in the current House-museum, the other is adjacent to or coincides with a part of the Bellincione house.

It should be remembered that the term "stufa" was used in the Middle Ages, and even in the Medici era, to refer to a place where people went to wash themselves, often public baths. Such places required a certain hydraulic capacity, and who knows if there are any traces or special pipes under the floors of the ancient buildings in Via San Martino. The Florentine sewerage system clearly has a channel that coincides with Via Santa Margherita.[101] It is also said that the original system dates back to "the time of Giano della Bella (1300)".[102]

Is there, then, an aquiferous reality teeming beneath Dante's neighbourhood? Personal fascination aside, it is certainly not our intention to propose a research project on the Florentine underground! Moreover, without any "help" from legends or popular traditions. But we can still talk about water.

---

[101] D. Ottati, *Il ventre di Firenze*, Olimpia, Firenze 1999, p. 17.

[102] These are the words of Fr. Bargellini, spoken during the meeting of the Municipal Council on 9 December 1966. See D. Ottati, *Il ventre di Firenze*, cit., p. 17.

COLLODI, NIPOTE
SUSSI
E BIRIBISSI

THE ARNO RIVER
(EPILOGUE)

But if the Dante's Neighborhood does not express, at least on a legendary level, the symbolic depth of the figures of its ancient inhabitants, where and how should we look for the Poet's soul?

Some Dante experts believe that the Poet is more closely linked to the Arno than to other places in the city, such as the Baptistery[103] or the Santa Margherita district.

The plaque that reads "per mezza Toscan si spazia un fiumicel che nasce in Falterona", placed at the beginning of the Lungarno Pecori Giraldi, is perhaps the most important of Dante's plaques, first of all because it is almost "outside", just as Dante is "kept outside", in exile.

Returning to the legend, the authentic initiatory passage probably has to do with the river and its "beyond". Roman Florence was born from the Arno and the need to cross it. The river was crossed in ancient times by Miniatus, who laid his head on the Mons Florentinus. It was crossed by Buondelmonte Buondelmonti, at the beginning of the feuds between Bianchi and Neri, who died under the statue of Mars, the ancient daimon of the Florentines. The statue itself was swept away by the river in the flood of 1333.[104]

Dante, "who will cross many rivers",[105] remembers

---

103 PARADISO, XXV, 7-9.

104 See E. Pecchioni (with L. Pecchioni), *La Statua di Marte*, in *Antiche Curiosità Fiorentine*, second edition, by Press & Archeos, Firenze 2016, p. 89.

105 See L. Conti Lapi interviewed in the documentary *Fiorendipità*, cit.

the Arno on several occasions, and in particular about his home: "io fui nato e cresciuto sovra 'l bel fiume d'Arno, alla Gran Villa", we also read above the door of the "Casa sua", in Via Dante Alighieri 2. The water and its flow tell us more about Dante than many walls and houses.

And so it is a pity that in Florence, for more than a century now, access to the river from the historic centre has been anything but spontaneous, apart from the famous "pescaia" and the parks that border the city. The affectionate contact felt in cities such as Paris, Turin and others does not take place in practice.[106]

We began our historical journey in the "Rione di Dante", ideally on a wooded early summer morning, in order to perceive something essential. We lingered for a long time on the ancient buildings around Piazza San Martino. We sought inspiration in the small churches and the great Badia. We have followed the hatred and the passion of the members of the historical families, we have looked into their towers and we have lost ourselves in the alleys created to contain these feelings. To the point of sinking, as far as possible, into the mystery of an incompleteness, its overlapping with an inaccessible legendary-initiatory tract.

The day is coming to an end, and soon the tourists will gather in some restaurant or hotel. Passages through the quarter become more sporadic. The Benedictine nuns in the nearby Badia say their vespers in perfect Italian, lifting the words with simplicity to the highest "circles".

---

[106] On the relationship between city and river, see Daniele Cardelli interviewed in the documentary *Fiorendipità*, cit.

We leave Florence for another evening, a night in which it is possible to get lost, if you wish, in an alleyway that is as romantic as it is dark.

What can we say, finally, about the soul of the city where Dante lived? we can perhaps say that it is no longer esperibile, or that it never was; that it has been washed away by political conflicts, floods, urban redevelopments and, finally, by capitalism, by the approaches of a world dominated by marketing.

But the "Neighbourhood" it is within us! It is a way of thinking about life in the city, a way of being with others that puts the soul at the centre.

And so, when we speak of the soul of Florence, we cannot help but think of the inspiration that carry within us: The Florentine Spirit itself. That quick and elegant possible "flicker", that upheaval, that structural restlessness that we have inherited from those who, time and again, raised this city, and therefore its citizenship, out of the mud.

But we think that this flicker was born even earlier: in the childhood of the poets who played in an alleyway within the walls of this city... where stones and values meet in a gentle ontological paradox.

And let us think of those who, between Santa Margherita and San Martino, received even more... as Luigi Stefani wrote: "who received that grace which gave him the incorruptibility of life and that sacred ferment which allowed him to drive love to an incessant sublimation".[107]

---

[107] L. Stefani, *Dante e la sua Chiesa*, cit., p. 16.

For all this, for this restlessness and fire, perhaps for this sublime perseverance which is more ours than many rational realities, the soul can never simply be in that house.

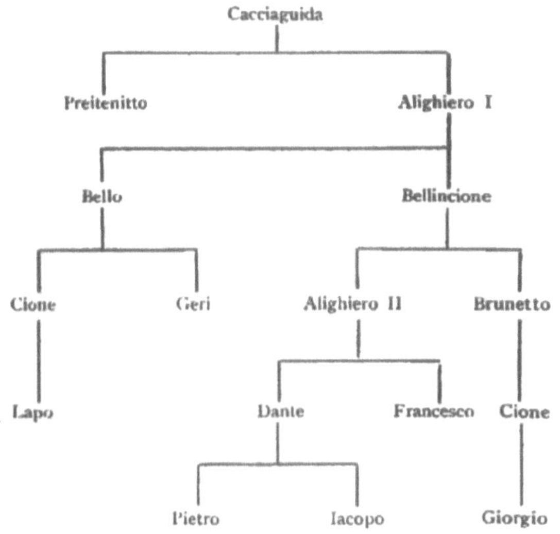

Simplified family tree of the Alighieri of San Martino
(G. Piranesi, 1915)

BIBLIOGRAPHY

AA.VV, *Della Casa di Dante. Relazione con documenti al consiglio generale del comune di Firenze*, Successori Le Monnier, Firenze 1865 (abbr. *Relazione*).

AA.VV. *La Casa di Dante Alighieri in Firenze. Relazione della Commissione istituita dalla Giunta Municipale del 17 marzo 1866 per compimento delle ricerche storiche sulla medesima*, Successori Le Monnier, Firenze 1869.

Barbi Michele-Piattoli Renato, *La Casa di Dante, in Studi Danteschi*, vol. XXII, Sansoni, Firenze 1938.

Barbi Michele, *D. Bortolan, Geri del Bello*, in *Bullettino della Società Dantesca Italiana*, n. s., II, 1895 (abbr. *Recensione a Bortolan*), pp. 67 e seg.

Barbi Michele, in *Bullettino della Società Dantesca Italiana*, v. XII, 1905, pp. 313 e seg.

Piero Bargellini, *Vita di Dante*, Vallecchi, Firenze 1964.

Piero Bargellini-Ennio Guarnieri, *Le strade di Firenze*, Bonechi, Firenze 1978.

Bortolan Domenico, *Geri Del bello*, ex-Cordelia, Venezia 1894.

Casanova Eugenio, Davidsohn Robert, *Nuovi documenti della famiglia di Dante*, in *Bullettino della Società Dantesca*, v. VII, 1898, pp. 97 e seg.

Davidshon Robert, *Storia di Firenze*, Sansoni, Firenze 1956, vol. IV.

Desideri Costa Leonia, *La Chiesa di S. Martino del Vescovo, l'Oratorio dei Buonomini e gli affreschi sulle opere di misericordia in Firenze presso le case degli Alighieri*, Tipocalcografia classica, Firenze 1942.

Dezzi Bardeschi Marco, *Il Monumento e il suo doppio*, Alinari, Firenze 1981.

Dorini Umberto, *Ancora dei beni rurali confiscati a Dante - le divise fatte dai figliuoli Pietro e Iacopo nel 1341 e 1347*, in *Bullettino della Società Dantesca*, vol. XIII, 1906, pp. 58.

Franchi Anna, *Le Case degli Alighieri*, in *La Lettura*, a. XXI, n. 10, ottobre 1921, pp. 742-746.

Formigli Giuseppe, *Guida per la citt^ di Firenze e i suoi contorni*, Forni, Firenze 1849

Imbriani Vittorio, *Studi Danteschi*, Sansoni, Firenze 1891.

Imbriani Vittorio, *Illustrazioni al capitolo dantesco del Centiloquio*, Marghieri, Napoli 1880.

Merejkowski Dimitri, *Dante*, Zanichelli, Bologna 1938.

Pagni Mario (a cura di), *Atlante archeologico di Firenze. Indagine storico-archeologica dalla preistoria all'alto Medioevo*, Polistampa, Firenze 2010.

Papini Giovanni, *Dante vivo*, Libreria Editrice Fiorentina, Firenze 1933.

Pecchioni Enio, *Antiche curiosità fiorentine*, Press & Archeos, Firenze 2010, seconda edizione, Firenze 2016.

Pecchioni Enio, *Piccola guida al Rione Dantesco*, stampato in proprio, Firenze 2010.

Pelli, Giuseppe Bencivenni, *Memorie per servire alla vita di Dante Alighieri ed alla storia della sua famiglia*, Piatti, Firenze 1823.

Piranesi Giorgio, *Le case degli Alighieri*, Lumachi, seconda edizione, Firenze 1905.

Piranesi Giorgio, *Sulla ubicazione e orientazione delle case degli Alighieri in Firenze*, stampato in proprio, Firenze 1905.

Piranesi Giorgio, in *Bullettino della Società Dantesca*, v. XIII, 1906, pp. 294-298 (abbr. *Autodifesa*).

Ottati Davis, *Il ventre di Firenze*, Olimpia, Firenze 1999, p. 17.

Richa Giuseppe, *Notizie istoriche delle chiese fiorentine*, Viviani, Firenze 1755.

Stefani Luigi, *Dante e la sua Chiesa*, Quaderni de «Lo Sprone», Firenze 1979

Video documentaries

Fiorendipità, storia e anima del Rione di Dante, Mediaframe, Firenze 2013.

La città dimenticata, storia archeologica della citt^ di Firenze, Film Documentari d'Arte, distr. Giunti, Firenze 1992.

Le ceneri di Jacques De Molay, Mediaframe, Firenze 2013.

CONTENT

Florence 2019